To Barbara,

A wonderous woman who pushes
life to its fullest and inspires
others to do the same.

With love and
        admiration
        Paul

Mrs. kitchen's cats

ken
ward's
world

Annick Press gratefully acknowledges
the support of The Canada Council and
the Ontario Arts Council.

Canadian Cataloguing in Publication Data

Ward, Ken, 1949–
  Mrs. Kitchen's cats

(Ken Ward's world)
Poems.
ISBN 1-55037-107-X

I. Title.   II. Series: Ward, Ken, 1949–   . Ken
Ward's world.

PS8595.A74M77 1990   jC811′.54   C90-095198-2
PZ8.3.W373Mr 1990

Distribution in Canada and the USA:
Firefly Books Ltd., 250 Sparks Avenue
North York, Ontario M2H 2S4

Printed and bound in Canada
by D.W. Friesen & Sons

Mrs. kitchen's cats

written and illustrated
by ken ward

annick press,
toronto, canada

**ducks and doves
are my favourite birds
i love their lovely
way with words
their gentle cooing
at the beach
their unpaid bills
all orangy peach**

Two elephants went walking
through the jungle green
they decided to go swimming
in the jungle stream
they floated on their backsides
their trunks up in the air
they swam about in figure-eights
this belly-flopping pair
they snorkeled and dog-paddled
oh, they tried to do it all
the butterfly, the breaststroke
and a slow australian crawl

my head is full of penguin talk

my legs are full of penguin walk

my eyes are full of penguin tears

my heart is of full of penguin fears

 my tail is full of penguin swing

my arms are full of penguin wing

my feet are full of penguin skid

could i be a  penguin kid?

mother had a dog

father had a cat

sister had a hamster

brother had a rat

uncle elmer had a horse

aunt alice had a bear

ernie had a pair of goats

a hereford and a hare

grandma had a partridge

granddad had a goose

i had an elephant

but it got loose

Alexander Graham Bell
inventor of the wishing well
loved to write but couldn't spell
Alexander Graham Bell

Alexander Graham Bell
ate his omelette, eggs and shell
had a secret he wouldn't tell
Alexander Graham Bell

Alexander Graham Bell
found his books by sense of smell
couldn't raise his voice to yell
Alexander Graham Bell

Alexander Graham Bell
brought a kite to show and tell
dreamt of farmers in the dell
Alexander Graham Bell

eggs so white

so very quiet

burst into

a chicken riot

hippos come in many colours
polka dots and stripes
solids, shades and ink band-aids
but never smoking pipes

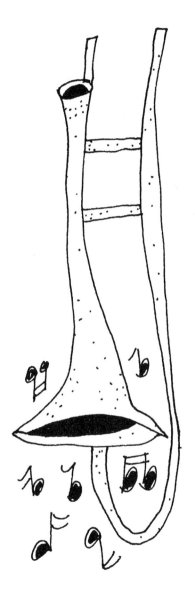

when i was **3**

i chased the cat

and slept at night

on an old straw mat

when i was **5**

and not so tall

i turned cartwheels

down the hall

when i was **6**

as i am now

i learned to milk

the goat, the cow

when i was **4**

i travelled alone

with a wink

in my pocket

and a slide trombone

you sing flowers
      i paint songs
you build towers
      i right wrongs
you talk fountains
      i eat dares
you move mountains
      i sleep bears
you cry colours
      i hide smiles
you dream mothers
      i sigh piles
you care worlds
      i care bunches
you watch colours
      i make lunches
you drink tea
      i drink too
you love me
      i love you

do you like my sunnyside? ah yes, but i do   you certainly are lucky to live in the sky blue clouds for a pillow the stars for a friend i hope that your happiness will never end

i have notebooks
filled with words
funny ideas
and laughing birds
pictures of lilies
poems of pigs
old phone numbers
and flying figs
notebooks full
of half-baked stories
cartoons and doodles
and morning glories
limerick lines
amazing phrases
drawings of firetrucks
going to blazes

i woke up this morning
my room full of stars
the moon on my dresser
my drawer full of mars
sunbeams were dancing
around my dazed head
an arc of a rainbow
lay aglow on my bed
comets came streaming
from out of my hat
two tons of jupiter
were squashing my cat
uranium chunks
lay scattered about
of the big dipper
a bit of the spout
my closet was filled
with saturnian rings
black holes and galaxies
and astroidy things
cobwebs from pluto
hung down from the clocks
an ocean of moonmist
had soaked through my socks
my room was so filled
with debris from deep space
that i knew i must move
to a much larger place

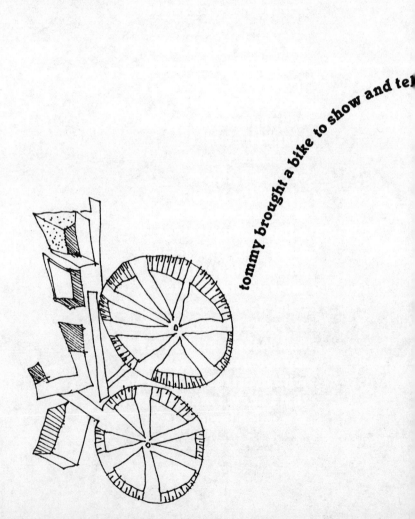

tommy brought a bike to show and tel

i wish i were
    a house of grass
a jungle hut
    where tigers pass
i wish i were
    the tigers' stripes
the playful sound
    of bamboo pipes

he rode it all around the room and rang the dinner bell

Dusty children, full of hope
    faintly smell of dogs and soap
    write no letters, eat sardines
    run along a fence that leans
    wade in water to their chins
    tell dark stories in dark coal bins
    watch the moon when no one sees
    gather sticks and stones and fleas

**adrift five days in a week
on a vegetable boat with a leek
fishing with skipping rope
for zucchinis and cantaloupe
navy beans in black sauce do i seek**

Gladys smells like rhubarb
warm peaches in december
frankincense and mirth
i really can't remember

henry smells like puddles
filled with piney timber
antique clocks on summer walls
i really can't remember

neddie smells like lemons
the summer warmth of embers
oatmeal coats on china bowls
i really can't remember

1 golden kangaroo
eating purple plums

2 scarlet orangutans
sitting on their bums

3 striped antelopes
leaping through the air

4 pink elephants
going to the fair

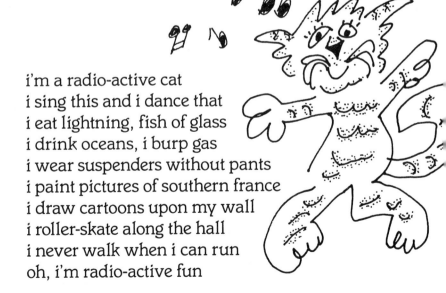

i'm a radio-active cat
i sing this and i dance that
i eat lightning, fish of glass
i drink oceans, i burp gas
i wear suspenders without pants
i paint pictures of southern france
i draw cartoons upon my wall
i roller-skate along the hall
i never walk when i can run
oh, i'm radio-active fun

mrs. kitchen's cats
don't wear no funny hats
they speak chinese
to all their fleas
and what's the use of that

mrs. kitchen's cats
wear socks and shoes with spats
they use the phone
when she's not home
they love long feline chats

mrs. kitchen's cats
sleep on wrestling mats
they romp and roll
to nat king cole
then drive her car with flats

mrs. kitchen's cats
play tag with cricket bats
they move the couch
in search of mouse
to eat with beans and rats

i wandered far when i was young i knew enough to hold my tongue i held it in my soft young head and nothing more was ever said

i love to eat peaches
in the rain
their fuzziness
ferments my brain
i love to eat cherries
on camping trips
they leave their redness
on my lips
i love to eat apples
juicy and round
i'm crazy for
that crunching sound

a kid and a fish

were walking to school

the fish made a wish

for a dip in a pool

the kid made a wish

for a sky full of rain

surely there's something

Snapdragon, snapdragon
why do you snap?
why is your kingdom
not on a map?
you look so adorable
can i sit on your lap?
snapdragon, snapdragon
why do you snap?

wrong with his brain

**children need
bright coloured clothes
sandcastle days
and a kiss on the nose**

Sweet william loved his tea
he drank it as a boy at sea
he shared it with the crew at three
sweet william loved his tea

sweet william loved his tea
he served it to his old auntie
she liked it very lemony
sweet william loved his tea

sweet william loved his tea
he balanced a cup upon his knee
he spilled it on the new settee
sweet william loved his tea

sweet william loved his tea
he slurped it for his sanity
he kept it in a chest with key
sweet william loved his tea

sweet william loved his tea
he gave it to his friends-to-be
they drank it in his memory
sweet william loved his tea

why do ducks
    love to dance
everytime
    they get the chance
they do the can-can
    all the time
ten ducks dancing
    in a line

i wear a suit made of tweed
turquoise, lemon and pink
i only wear it saturdays
at the skating rink
the kids all laugh, i do not care
when they giggle and twitter
and whisper and stare
cos i love my suit
i love to skate
saturdays i dream of being great

i love my gramma more than gold
she loves me more than tea
and even though i'm much too large
i sit upon her knee

i love my gramma more than milk
she loves me like the sun
she lets me eat with chopsticks
oh, she's a lot of fun

i love my gramma more than cats
she loves me more than mice
we like to go to bingo
and drink our beer with ice

i love my gramma more than soaps
she loves me more than sports
we go for walks on winter nights
and talk about our hopes

i love my gramma more than school
she loves me more than boats
we like to travel to the zoo
in our matching coats

i love my gramma more than stew
she loves me more than roast
we like to talk about the world
while eating peas on toast

i love my gramma more than red
she loves me more than green
i like to listen to her jokes
about the king and queen

you dance on a rainbow the rain's gone away

shoes filled with colours do stay for the day

I used to know a scarecrow
who was scared as scared can be
so i spent my days
in the carrot patch
just to keep him company

how much does a shadow weigh?
if you ask it, will a shadow play?
can shadows hear, what do they think
of rambling roses, red and pink?
are shadows softer in the heat?
do shadows ever want to eat?
shadows seem so everywhere
why do shadows stand and stare?
they never speak, they're often mute
do shadows ever give a hoot?

who can fly above the sand?

Kitty had an accident
she fell out of a tree
everyone agreed it was
a real catastrophe

the steps   of   the stairs   are thoughts   that are cares

who can? a peli can

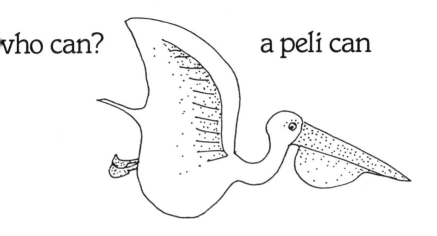

dad has big boots
tall and long

i get lost
when i put them on

a bookworm lives
**   inside a book**
never giving
**   it a look**
a bookworm eats it
**   word for word**
from zanzibar
**   to absurd**

I am very, very old
and these are some
    of the things i know
i know the earth is flat, not round
i know where panda bears are found
i know a story five nights long
i know an egyptian birthday song
i know who loves you
    when you're sad
i know why dinosaurs ate my dad
i know how to call a moose
and how to get down
from a goose

little chickens
from peru
typing letters
two by two
soliloquies
prose and poems
to read to children
in their homes
drinking whiskey
and eating hay
inventing stories
ten a day
they hunt and peck
peck and crow
writing novels
row on row
these little birds
are so unique
from their classic tales
to their bookish beaks

My dog is dead
the fridge is broke
little tommy tucker
gave the cat a poke
i can't spell mathamatics
my sister wrecked the car
on her way to paris
she hit a falling star
the sun's too hot
my fish can't swim
my friend's in dutch
and i'm with him
dad lost his job
to a college grad
uncle albert got toasted
on a heating pad
grandma moses
is up a tree
the t.v. is cracked
too bad to see
this family is lucky
that cows can't fly
but we'll get through
somehow, by and by

i have secrets, made of ice
  i have tunnels, china bound
i have rockets, filled with rice
  i have laughter, without sound
i have raincoats, made of mist
  i have shoes, two black brothers
i have wings, angel kissed
  i have seasons, nature's mothers
i have visions, sapphire eyes
  i have mercury, summer blood
i have wisdom, sadder sighs
  i have rivers, flowing flood
i have rainbows, golden stages
  i have crimson, blues and green
i have freedom, words on pages
  i have lives i've never seen

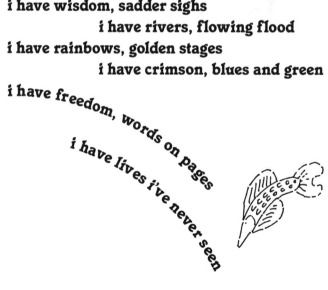

i lost ten pounds
down the drain

i had a bath

and washed my brain

time is the hands
of the clock on the wall

time is a clock
with no hands at all

time is a minute
an hour, a day

time is not knowing
when to come in from play

if i owned a store, what would i sell

a piano for midgets, with an ice-cream bell

ten winks in a bottle, perfume from malay

two tigers purring at the end of the day

a bowl full of marbles, a barrel of fish

hope wrapped in paper and tied with a wish

shoes lined in velvet, feathers and wool

crystaline icicles, deliciously cool

carousel horses, a new sun for the sky

a new kid in school, exceedingly shy

bats in a belfry, mice underground

ebony bowling balls, not quite round

parrots with feathers down to their bills

sneakers and cookies and pictures of hills

calliopes, cantalopes, cartoons and hair

pulled from a panther with the greatest of care

bottles of ginger-beer, single shoe laces

pillows for pandas with short furry faces

turnips, blue paper, pots full of rain

a purple caboose from the end of a train

the bark of a dog, a seal and three trees

a complete set of dickens without any c's

moonbeams in season, bicycle brakes

roosters and raisins for rooraisin cakes

fat ballet teachers in colorful tights

oranges and apricots and japanese kites

pineapple patches, pumpkin stew

red sand from the desert, rhinoceros glue

rare asian unicorns, purples and pinks

sowpony saddles and kitchen sinks

mrs. green was never seen
wearing high-heeled shoes
mr. red stood on his head
because he had the blues

trombone player
breakfast late

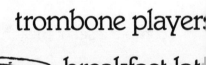

i am sitting in a teacup a book upon my head

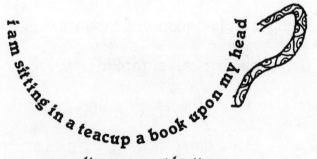

spreading peanut butter
on the downside of my bread

The platypus was designed
for life in the water
she looks like a duck
but swims like an otter

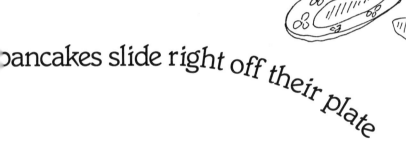

pancakes slide right off their plate

heather has her bubble bath
in the kitchen sink
cups and saucers
pots and pans

clink, clink, clink

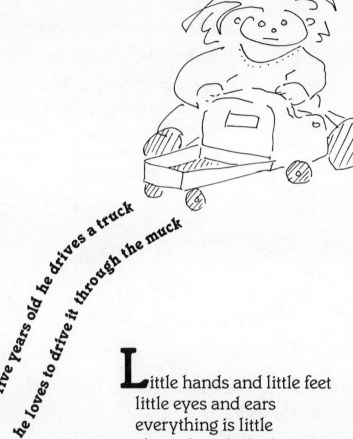

ralph's five years old he drives a truck
he loves to drive it through the muck

Little hands and little feet
little eyes and ears
everything is little
about these little dears
little mouths, little legs
little wee behinds
everything is little
except their little minds

i am living in a box
my hair is longer than a fox
with dirty face and dirty sox
i am living in a box

i am living in a shed
with no covers, with no bed
a newspaper hat upon my head
i am living in a shed

i am living on the street
two soleless shoes upon my feet
in winter shivering without heat
i am living on the street

i am living in a car
no strings upon my old guitar
my breakfast is a chocolate bar
i am living in a car

i am living in a can
garbage piling up like sand
hand-to-mouth and mouth-to-hand
i am living in a can

i am living in a crate
my only warmth a subway grate
a tattered life, my unseen fate
i am living in a crate

alexander the great was never late

he ate all the veggies upon his plate

things begin and then they end in the midd

noah's ark

sprung a leak

he patched it up
with a pelican beak

Eleven strange flavours, each one rare
one that tastes like witches' hair
one that tastes like funhouse laughs
one that tastes like short giraffes
one that tastes like ostrich plumes
one that tastes like dusty rooms
one that tastes like jungle cries
one that tastes like summer sighs
one that tastes like snowy nights
one that tastes like mosquito bites
one that tastes like kids at play
one that tastes like yesterday

a lifelong friend

monkeys annoy me
they're really quite rude
they heckle and jeckle
and throw up their food
i'm irked by the aardvarks
they're really quite boring
they walk around slowly
and i can't stand their snoring
rhinos torment me
they plague me no end
with their thick leather covers
and a horn to defend
i'm pestered by panthers
they snarl, spit and prowl
they hinder my thinking
cos' i'm scared of their growl
giraffes worry me
they're really too tall

they nettle and tease me
and what if they fall
ostriches disquiet me
with their heads in the ground
porcupines vex me
they're sharp and they're round
i'm molested by butterflies
insects and grubs
when buffalos beset me
i hide in the shrubs
kangaroo hopping
drives me insane
i'm ruffled by racoons
picking my brain
hyenas harangue me
they threaten my life
they laugh at my haircut,
my legs and my wife

i am afraid  of water skiis

aardvark bites and rare disease

deep, dark closets and spikey plants

 dragon's breath and army ants

near-sighted elephants and night-owl hoots

sharp, silver spurs on cowboy boots

quicksand pits and leaky boats

dentist smiles and sneaky goats

cobwebs in basements full of mice

snakes in tall grass, falling ice

 paper cuts and vinegar vats

meteor showers and baseball bats

warts and wars and cross-eyed kings

yes, i am afraid of all of these things

Emily doolittle
was on a walk
she met a parade
that wouldn't talk
the elephants roared
the clowns all laughed
emily smiled
the streets giraffed

t v kids

have no brains

pop-corn breath

and rear-end pains

a little bowl of sleep
before the baby goes to bed

a little bowl of sleep
to put some dreams inside her head

a little bowl of sleep
with a piece of cheese and bread

a little bowl of sleep
before the baby goes to bed